INDEX

The Islamic State

The Islamic State of Iraq and the Levant (ISIL)—formerly known as al-Qa'ida in Iraq and Islamic State of Iraq—was established in April 2004 by long-time Sunni extremist Abu Mus'ab al-Zarqawi, who the same year pledged his group's allegiance to Usama Bin Ladin. ISIL targeted Coalition forces and civilians using high-profile tactics such as vehicle-borne improvised explosive devices (VBIEDs), suicide bombers, and hostage executions, to pressure foreign countries and companies to leave Iraq, push Iraqis to stop supporting the United States and the Iraqi Government, and attract additional cadre to its ranks.

Following al-Zarqawi's death in June 2006, ISIL's new leader, Abu Ayyub al-Masri, announced in October 2006 the formation of the Islamic State of Iraq, led by Iraqi national Abu 'Umar al-Baghdadi, in an attempt to politicize the group's terrorist activities and place an "Iraqi face" on their efforts.

In 2007, ISIL's continued targeting and repression of Sunni civilians in Iraq caused a widespread backlash—known as the Sunni Awakening—against the group. The development of the Awakening Councils—composed primarily of Sunni tribal and local community leaders—coincided with a surge in Coalition and Iraqi Government operations, resulting in a decreased attack tempo beginning in mid-2007.

ISIL's current leader, Abu Bakr al-Baghdadi, assumed power following the death of both Abu Ayyub al-Masri and Abu 'Umar al-Baghdadi in April 2010. Under his authority, the group has continued conducting high-profile attacks across Iraq. ISIL has expanded its ranks through prison breaks and integration of fighters drawn to the Syrian conflict.

In April 2013, Abu Bakr al-Baghdadi publicly declared the group's presence in Syria under the name ISIL and that ISIL had founded the al-Nusrah Front in Syria. Al-Nusrah Front in June 2013 publicly pledged allegiance to al-Qa'ida leader Ayman al-Zawahiri. The disagreement and ISIL's hardline ideology caused a backlash in Syria. ISIL rejected al-Nusrah Front, Syrian opposition enemies, and al-Qa'ida's efforts to force the group to leave Syria.

In February 2014, al-Qa'ida publicly stated ISIL was no longer a branch of al-Qa'ida, a status the group had held since 2004. ISIL in April 2014 responded to the disavowal by publicly attacking al-Qa'ida as being unfit for Usama Bin Ladin's legacy and stating that ISIL was a better example for jihadists. Major ISIL-led efforts to overthrow the Iraqi Government erupted in June 2014, freeing prisoners and gaining access to more weapons and vehicles usable in Iraq or Syria. In late June 2014, ISIL declared the establishment of an Islamic caliphate under the name the "Islamic State" and called for all Muslims to pledge allegiance to the group.

Background

The evolution of the group that calls itself the "Islamic State" (IS) is best understood as an outcome of both design and accident. It is an outcome of design because the group's territorial gains and governance, according to what it believes to be Islamic teachings, were part of the vision of its founder, Abu Mus'ab al-Zarqawi, since at least 1999.

In this respect, it is critical to appreciate the differences between IS and al-Qa'ida (AQ). For while AQ considered itself as an anti-establishment global force of "jihadis without borders," al-Zarqawi's vision was one of building an establishment, a vision that his successors have sought to translate into a reality. Indeed, the Iraq-based group learned from some of its past failures, including the mistakes of its founder.

But the IS is also an outcome of accidents that allowed the group to exploit the militant landscape in Syria as well as the politics of sectarianism that adversely affected Iraq's Arab Sunnis. To borrow from Machiavelli's vocabulary, the leaders of the IS did not achieve their recent successes only through their skills (virtu), but luck (fortuna) also played a considerable part in what they achieved.

The killing of al-Zarqawi in June 2006 did not cause his successors to give up on his plan of building a society (mujtama'); indeed, they developed more ambitious designs. Abu Hamza al-Muhajir succeeded al-Zarqawi, and his initial statement suggests that he saw his group to be loyal to AQ, assuring Bin Ladin that "we are at your beck and call and at your disposal."

Yet within four months, Abu Hamza pledged allegiance to Abu `Umar al-Baghdadi's newly formed group the "Islamic State of Iraq" (ISI), thereby submitting the "army of al-Qa'ida," as Abu Hamza put it, to the authority of the ISI. It is reported that both Abu Hamza and Abu 'Umar had trained in

Afghanistan and joined al-Zarqawi's group in Iraq. It is also reported that it was Abu 'Umar al-Baghdadi who served as the intellectual engine of the ISI.

If it is true that he was the head of the Advisory Council that al-Zarqawi joined, then his influence on the Iraq-based group predates his assumption of its leadership in 2006. The so-called state did not want to limit its activities to militancy and in April 2007 it announced the appointment of ten ministers, including ministers for health, oil, agriculture, and fisheries. In other words, the ISI conceived of itself to be in the business of governance. The declaration of a state in 2006 did not meet the approval of AQ, and judging by internal communiqués, AQ's leaders were highly critical of Abu Hamza and Abu 'Umar. According to a statement released by al-Zawahiri in May 2014, the proclamation of the ISI was made without any consultation with AQ's leadership, not even with Bin Ladin.

Al-Zawahiri seems keen to highlight AQ's displeasure with Abu Hamza and Abu 'Umar, so much so that he cited an anonymous letter highly critical of both leaders that was captured during the raid that killed Bin Ladin.

The letter that al-Zawahiri cites highlights the "political mistakes" of Abu 'Umar, and refers to him and Abu Hamza as "extremists," "repulsive," and "lack[ing] wisdom." U.S. and Iraqi forces killed Abu `Umar and Abu Hamza in April 2010, and Abu Bakr al-Baghdadi assumed the leadership of the ISI and has been in charge of the Iraq-based group since then. The challenge that the declaration of the ISI posed to AQ, however, did not end with their death. Two serious implications resulted as a consequence of Abu Hamza's pledge of allegiance to Abu 'Umar.

The first concerns the very notion of declaring an "Islamic state": this entails elaborate conditions, including providing security to the populace residing in the territory of the "state" and making jihadists accountable to good governance, an accountability that the ISI could hardly deliver at that stage, not least given the occupation of Iraq by U.S. forces at the time. It is for such reasons that Bin Ladin mocked al-Qa'ida in the Arabian Peninsula (AQAP) for wanting to declare an Islamic state in Yemen, and urged Somalia's al-Shabaab not to go that route.

Indeed, al-Qa'ida's statement disowning the ISIL does not admit that it represents a "state"; instead, it refers to the ISIL as the "group" that calls itself a "state." The criticism is made more apparent when the statement derisively remarks that "we do not hasten to declare emirates and states...that we impose on people, then declare whoever disapproves of such entities to be a rebel (kharij) [against whom it is lawful to fight]."

The second serious implication pertains to Abu Hamza's oath to Abu 'Umar when he pledged, "I hereby enlist under your direct leadership twelve thousand fighters who constitute the army of al-Qa'ida." Did the ISI cease to be under the leadership of AQ in 2006, and, indeed, did the pledge by Abu Hamza effectively subordinate Bin Ladin's authority to that of al-Baghdadi? Of course, Bin Ladin never pledged allegiance to Abu 'Umar, and according to al-Zawahiri's May 2014 letter, Abu Hamza wrote to the leadership of AQ to assure them that the group continued to consider itself to be part of AQ.

Nevertheless, because Bin Ladin did not go public and discredit the group, the ISI became a fait accompli "state," acting without consultation with AQ and even against its directions. In an internal communiqué dated early 2011, the American jihadist Adam Gadahn advised the leadership that "it is necessary that al-Qa'ida publicly announces that it severs its organizational ties with the Islamic State of Iraq, and [to make known] that the relationship between its leadership and that of the State [i.e., ISI] have not existed for several years, and that the decision to declare a State was taken without consultation with the leadership, and this [ill-considered] innovative affirmation (qarar ijtihadi) led to divisions among jihadists and their supporters inside and outside Iraq."

Why did it take so long for AQ to disown ISI/ISIL publicly if the problems between them began in 2005 and worsened in 2006? In April 2013, al-Baghdadi unilaterally proclaimed the founding of the ISIL by declaring a merger between his group and that of Jabhat al-Nusra (JN) in Syria. JN, it should be noted, was the first jihadist group to emerge in Syria in January 2012, and in its nascent phase, it was praised even by non-jihadists for its effective conduct on the battlefield, and its dealings with the populace.

It was not organic to the Syrian revolution; instead, its members had fought alongside the ISI in Iraq and their move to Syria was initially funded by ISI.48 The leader of JN, Abu Muhammad al-Julani, publicly rejected the merger and pledged allegiance directly to al-Zawahiri. In June 2013, al-Zawahiri intervened, annulling the merger and therefore the very concept of the ISIL, and appointed Abu Khalid al-Suri – who had fought in Afghanistan and was closely connected to the jihadi strategist Abu Mus'ab al-Suri and Ayman al-Zawahiri –50 a member of the Syrian militant group Harakat Ahrar al-Sham, to serve as an arbitrator between the two groups.

Several things may have caused al-Baghdadi to make this unilateral decision: it is possible that he was envious of JN's stardom in the jihadist world, and he wanted to make it known to the world that gratitude is owed to his group; it is also possible that he was worried about his investment in JN, seeing that it was collaborating with militant groups whose agenda was nationalist rather than jihadist; or he believed that the time was ripe to expand his "state" into Syria. Judging by what happened later, expanding the "state" would not only make his divorce from AQ public; it would also fulfill the modus operandi that al-Zarqawi and his successors had envisaged for the jihadist landscape. That is to say, the jihadism of the ISIL/IS is not designed simply to fight against the perceived unjust global establishment, as it was with AQ, but is in fact aimed to create a just establishment and deliver what al-Zarqawi had started.

Al-Zawahiri may have sensed that the merger that al-Baghdadi was imposing on JN amounted to a coup against AQ, hence his intervention to annul the ISIL. Before long, the public dispute developed into a bloody conflict, particularly starting in December 2013, when the ISIL kidnapped and then killed Abu Sa'd al-Hadrami, the leader of JN in the Syrian province of al-Raqqa.54 It is not clear which side initiated the transgression: although the ISIL received the lion's share of criticisms in the mainstream media, it is also the case that statements by the ISIL in early January 2014 suggest that its members were being harassed, imprisoned, and constrained in their movements by other militant groups in Syria.

According to al-Baghdadi, the changes in the name of the group occurred to reflect the group's "[higher level of] development and nobility of aspiration." Following this line of logic, now that the name is ecumenical with the dropping of geographical references, we can expect no further changes to the name the "Islamic State." But as President Barack Obama remarked, "ISIL is certainly not a state" according to international law.

Nevertheless, while Obama's statement is designed to cut the group down to size and highlight that it is nothing more than a terrorist organization, the group projects itself otherwise. To be sure, the IS does not seek membership in the United Nations to be part of the global community of nation-states. Indeed, it believes the world order to be illegitimate and seeks to redraw today's world map and create a global Islamic state, a caliphate, akin to that which predates the modern state system. Accordingly, the group is intent on pursuing the acquisition of additional territories beyond Iraq and Syria.

Indeed, in his address on the occasion of the start of the holy month of Ramadan, the designated caliph promises that if the "soldiers of IS" remain united and commit themselves to being the "guardians of religion," they "shall conquer Rome and seize the earth."

Yet from a legal perspective, why should the "Islamic state" of 2014 be any different from that which was proclaimed in 2006 (i.e., the Islamic State of Iraq) or that which was announced in 2013 (i.e., ISIL)? One would think that the intent of establishing an Islamic state is intrinsically universal, an issue that the jihadist pundit Abu al-Fadl Madi, an opponent of the IS, highlighted. He questioned whether there is anything legally meaningful about it and forewarned that even a "limited air bombing campaign could deny this caliphate all its resources."

It is perhaps more important to ask what the IS could deliver by way of outcomes. An internal communiqué to the ISI designed to present an internal critique of the Iraq-based group in the years 2006–2007 suggests that the announcement of a state was used by many of the group's leaders "to cover up their weaknesses (in the military and security [domains]) and [they] to convincing themselves and others that they should [focus on] building a state and its institutions without paying due attention to military and security matters." The author laments that the announcement of the state caused that generation of leaders to be "deluded" by a supposed power in the form of a state.

In his mind, this led to a complacency such that "we [i.e., ISI] switched roles [with the Americans]," and "we virtually became an organized army whose movements are known ... to everyone while America turned into guerillas working to assassinate the leaders and the jihadist elites ... we lost the cities, then the villages and [even] the desert became a dangerous shelter ... and found ourselves in a closed circle." What has gone right for the ISI since then? And will the change of name lead to a different outcome this time?

If the first generation of the ISI fighters found themselves in 2007 and 2008 lost in the desert and in a "closed circle" after they were rejected by Arab Sunnis, why would today's IS fighters be in control of Sunni-majority territories in Iraq and Syria? Even though the Iraq-based group sees itself as championing the

Sunni creed, the group's relationship with Iraq's Arab Sunnis, including militant Sunni groups, has been nothing short of tumultuous. Numerous internal documents attest to this history.

One such document by the ISI portrays Iraqi Sunnis (ansar) to have presented a challenge from the start, largely because they did not share the same ideology. "Most of the brothers," the document relates, "have severe difficulty reciting the Qur'an and understanding its meaning ... often deferring to the head of the tribe in matters of war and peace."

They seem to have joined the ranks of jihadists "so that they may secure their daily bread ... without having the sincere intention to take up arms and fight against the infidels and the apostates."

It appears that al-Zarqawi's group was constrained by the Arab Sunnis' lack of cooperation. In a document dated 18 February 2005, al-Zarqawi's group states that it is disappointed to see that some tribal members "stand as a stumbling block in the path of jihad and have taken to obstructing the work of jihadis." It goes on to threaten that whoever stands in the way of jihadists or speaks ill of them shall see that "the swords of jihadists shall respond with an appropriate punishment so that [the fate of the culprit] may serve as a lesson to others."

Other internal documents reveal that the tension progressively expanded to include militant Iraqi Sunni groups who had once sided with the jihadists believing them to be fighting to repel U.S. occupation from Iraq. In a document dated 13 May 2007, the ISI justifies its killing of twelve leaders from the groups al-Jaysh al-Islami, Ansar al-Sunna, and Jaysh al-Mujahidin, asserting that the operation is a "natural outcome resulting from the conduct of this 'rebel group'" (al-zumra al-baghiya). The author explains that the problem had begun at least a year earlier and suggests that these groups attract mostly former members of "the apostate state."

In a document by al-Jaysh al-Islami, the group highlights, among other things, what it considers to be the extremism of ISI, its threats to shed the blood of those who do not pledge allegiance to it, its attempt "to eliminate the jihad of those who do not follow [ISI]." In the same document, al-Jaysh al-Islami calls on Bin Ladin to dissociate his organization from the actions of the ISI and correct its way.

Despite the tumultuous history the group experienced with Arab Sunnis, the success of ISIL/IS in mid-2014 to acquire territory in Iraq is not divorced from the period that precedes it. Two key factors allowed the ISI/ISIL/IS to exploit events affecting Arab Sunnis to its advantage. On the Iraqi side, it was able to exploit a parallel domestic struggle concerning the sectarian politics that alienated Arab Sunnis. On the Syrian side, in late December 2013 and early January 2014, the ISIL forces suffered the loss of their strongholds in western Syria at the hands of other rebel groups.

This forced them to consolidate themselves in the territories in eastern Syria bordering Iraq. By that time, Arab Sunnis in Iraq had given up on a peaceful solution with the Maliki government and turned against government forces, creating a fragile security environment that was ultimately exploited by the ISIL. As will be discussed below, it is either that the ISIL's plan could predict with precision how the events were about to unfold, or that the events, particularly in Iraq, presented the ISIL with an outcome that was too good to be true.

While countless reasons may be enumerated for the ISIL's exploitation of events that affected Arab Sunnis in Iraq, one cannot avoid highlighting two key structural causes related to the politics of sectarianism in Iraq, in addition to the Iraqi government's response to the peaceful demonstrations calling for political reform that started in late 2012. The two structural causes concern (1) the political sectarianism that was introduced by the 2005 constitution, and (2) the forced displacement (tahjir qasri) of people on the basis of religious affiliation to create a demographic map along sectarian lines. On the constitutional level, prior to the fall of Saddam Hussein in 2003, while many Iraqis had suffered under his dictatorship, his reign was secular, promoting his loyalists and brutally eliminating his opponents, regardless of sects or ethnicity.

Yet it was Arab Sunnis who bore the lion's share of sectarianism that followed the U.S. invasion of Iraq. Saad Jawad, a scholar of Iraqi politics, argues that the United States "reduc[ed] the Iraqi state to a collection of Shi'as, Sunnis, Kurds and other minorities," an approach that was ultimately translated into "the new constitution emphasis[ing] differences and divisive issues rather than focusing on the uniting elements of Iraqi society."

Jawad remarks that "sectarian affiliations had never been mentioned in an Iraqi constitution," whereas the new constitution affirmed the distinction between sects and sidelined the Arab Sunni population whose representatives sought to emphasize the Arab identity of the state.

The Abu Sayyaf Group

The Abu Sayyaf Group (ASG) is the most violent of the Islamic separatist groups operating in the southern Philippines and claims to promote an independent Islamic state in western Mindanao and the Sulu Archipelago. Split from the Moro National Liberation Front in the early 1990s, the group currently engages in kidnappings for ransom, bombings, assassinations, and extortion, and has had ties to Jemaah Islamiyah (JI). The ASG operates mainly in Basilan, Sulu, and Tawi-Tawi Provinces in the Sulu Archipelago and has a presence on Mindanao. Members also occasionally travel to Manila.

2000, an ASG faction kidnapped 21 persons—including 10 Westerners—from a Malaysian resort, and, in May 2001, the ASG kidnapped three US citizens and 17 Filipinos from a resort in Palawan, Philippines, later murdering several of the hostages, including one US citizen. In June 2002, one of the two remaining hostages was killed in a crossfire between Philippine soldiers and the ASG. On 27 February 2004, members of ASG leader Khadafi Janjalani's faction bombed a ferry in Manila Bay, killing 116, and on 14 February 2005 they perpetrated simultaneous bombings in the cities of Manila, General Santos, and Davao, killing at least eight and injuring about 150. In 2006, Janjalani's faction relocated to Sulu, where it joined forces with local ASG supporters who are providing shelter to fugitive JI members from Indonesia.

In July 2007, members of the ASG and the Moro Islamic Liberation Front engaged a force of Philippine marines on Basilan Island, killing 14. In November 2007, a motorcycle bomb exploded outside the Philippine Congress, killing a Congressman and three staff members. While there was no definitive claim of responsibility, three suspected ASG members were arrested during a subsequent raid on a safe house. In January 2009, the ASG kidnapped three International Red Cross workers in Sulu province, holding one of the hostages for six months. Philippine marines in February 2010 killed Albader Parad, one of the ASG's most violent sub-commanders, on Jolo Island. In 2011, the ASG kidnapped several individuals and held them for ransom. In February 2012, a Philippine military airstrike against a terrorist encampment on Jolo Island killed senior ASG leader Gumbahali Jumdail, also known as Dr. Abu.In March 2013, the ASG released an Australian citizen the group had held hostage for fifteen months. In June 2014, Philippine authorities arrested senior ASG figure ASG Khair Mundos in metro

The Taliban

The Taliban is a Sunni Islamist nationalist and pro-Pashtun movement founded in the early 1990s that ruled most of Afghanistan from 1996 until October 2001. The movement's founding nucleus—the word "Taliban" is Pashto for "students"—was composed of peasant farmers and men studying Islam in Afghan and Pakistani madrasas, or religious schools. The Taliban found a foothold and consolidated their strength in southern Afghanistan.

By 1994, the Taliban had moved their way through the south, capturing several provinces from various armed factions who had been fighting a civil war after the Soviet-backed Afghan government fell in 1992. The Taliban's first move was to institute a strict interpretation of Qur'anic instruction and jurisprudence. In practice, this meant often merciless policies on the treatment of women, political opponents of any type, and religious minorities.

In the years leading up to the 11 September 2001 attacks in the United States, the Taliban provided a safe haven for al-Qa'ida. This gave al-Qa'ida a base in which it could freely recruit, train, and deploy terrorists to other countries. The Taliban held sway in Afghanistan until October 2001, when they were routed from power by the US-led campaign against al-Qa'ida.

The Afghan Taliban's leader is Mullah Mohammad Omar, who was the president of Afghanistan during the Taliban's rule. The US Government is offering a $10 million reward for information leading to his capture.

The Afghan Taliban are responsible for most insurgent attacks in Afghanistan. In January 2014, the group staged a suicide and small-arms attack on the popular Lebanese Taverna restaurant in Kabul, killing 21 people, including three Americans, marking one of the deadliest attacks against Western civilians in Kabul since 2001. In a one-week span in March 2014, the Taliban conducted four high-profile attacks in Kabul city, culminating in a 28 March attack on a heavily guarded guesthouse in Kabul for employees of a US aid group. The targeted guesthouse was next to a Christian charity and day-care center that may have been the intended target. The next day, the Taliban conducted an attack on the headquarters of Afghanistan's election commission with rockets and automatic rifles, following an attack on the provincial election office earlier that week. On 20 March, the Taliban attacked Kabul's luxurious Serena Hotel, killing nine civilians who were all shot at point-blank range by four insurgents armed with small pistols smuggled inside.

Al-Nusrah Front

Al-Nusrah Front is one of the most capable al-Qa'ida-affiliated groups operating in Syria during the ongoing conflict. The group in January 2012 announced its intention to overthrow Syrian President Bashar al-Asad's regime, and since then has mounted hundreds of insurgent-style and suicide attacks against regime and security service targets across the country. The group is committed not only to ousting the regime, but also seeks to expand its reach regionally and globally. Initially, al-Nusrah Front did not publicize its links to al-Qa'ida in Iraq or Pakistan.

The Islamic State of Iraq and the Levant (ISIL) played a significant role in founding the group. ISIL predecessor organizations used Syria as a facilitation hub and transformed this facilitation and logistics network into an organization capable of conducting sophisticated explosives and firearms attacks. ISIL leaders since the beginning of al-Nusrah Front's participation in the conflict provided their facilitation hub with personnel and resources, including money and weapons.

During 2013, al-Nusrah Front and ISIL were consumed by a public rift stemming from ISIL leader Abu Bakr al-Baghdadi's April 2013 statement announcing the creation of ISIL and claiming the merger of both groups. Al-Nusrah Front and ISIL have strategies for Syria, and a public merger between them probably would have undermined al-Nusrah Front's autonomy in the country. In April 2013, al-Nusrah Front's leader, Abu Muhammad al-Jawlani, pledged allegiance to al-Qa'ida leader Ayman al-Zawahiri.

During early 2014, the rift between al-Nusrah Front and ISIL—in which ISIL has openly accused al-Qa'ida senior leaders of deviating from what it perceives as the correct jihadist path—has taken place not just on the ground but in social media as well. Al-Nusrah Front's leaders probably have learned lessons from members' previous experiences in Iraq and have sought to win over the Syrian populace by providing parts of the country with humanitarian assistance and basic civil services. Several Syria-based armed opposition groups cooperate and fight alongside Sunni extremist groups, including al-Nusrah Front, and are dependent upon them for expertise, training, and weapons. Al-Nusrah Front has managed to seize territory, including military bases and infrastructure in northern Syria.

The group's cadre is predominately composed of Syrian nationals, many of whom are veterans of previous conflicts, including the Iraq war. Thousands of fighters from around the world have traveled to Syria since early 2012 to support oppositionist groups, and some fighters aspire to connect with al-Nusrah Front and other extremist groups. Several Westerners have joined al-Nusrah Front, including a few who have died in suicide operations. Western government officials have raised concerns that capable individuals with extremist contacts and battlefield experience could return to their home countries to commit violent acts. An al-Nusrah Front attack in May 2014—the first known suicide bombing by an American in Syria—targeted regime personnel, highlighting the involvement of US persons in the conflict.

Ansar Bayt al-Maqdis

Ansar Bayt al-Maqdis (ABM) is the most active and capable terrorist group operating in Egypt. ABM shares al-Qa'ida's ideology and seeks the destruction of Israel, the establishment of an Islamic caliphate in the Sinai Peninsula, and the implementation of sharia. The group is based in the Sinai but since fall 2013 has expanded its operational reach into Egypt's Nile Valley.

ABM emerged in 2011 when it claimed responsibility for a cross-border attack into southern Israel from the Sinai. Since 2011, ABM has carried out additional cross-border attacks, launched rocket attacks against Israel, and repeatedly bombed the gas pipeline in the Sinai that supplies natural gas to Israel and Jordan.

Following the August 2013 crackdown by Egyptian security forces on those protesting the ouster of President Muhammad Mursi, ABM launched a campaign of attacks against Egyptian government and security targets. ABM since then has claimed responsibility for several of the highest-profile and sophisticated attacks in Egypt, including an attempted assassination of the Egyptian Minister of the Interior, the downing of an Egyptian military helicopter in the Sinai with a surface-to-air missile, and several deadly vehicle-borne improvised explosive device attacks against Egyptian security installations.

ABM for the first time demonstrated its willingness to target civilians when it claimed responsibility for a suicide bombing on a tourist bus in the Sinai in February 2014, though ABM described the attack as targeting Egyptian economic interests. ABM claimed responsibility for another suicide bombing in South Sinai in early May 2014 that injured Egyptian workers.

ABM has not made explicit threats against the West or Western targets in its official propaganda. However, the group views the West, and the United States in particular, as supporters of Israel and Egypt and expresses anti-Western sentiment in its rhetoric. Various social media accounts claiming association with the group have posted threats to US and other Western targets, although ABM has repeatedly denied a social media presence.

Egyptian security officials in late May 2014 claimed to have killed ABM's leader—whom they identified as Shadi al-Mani'—but ABM denied the individual was the leader of the group or that he had been killed

Al-Shabaab

The Harakat al-Shabaab al-Mujahidin—commonly known as al-Shabaab—was the militant wing of the Somali Council of Islamic Courts that took over most of southern Somalia in the second half of 2006. Despite the group's defeat by Somali and Ethiopian forces in 2007, al-Shabaab—a clan-based insurgent and terrorist group—has continued its violent insurgency in southern and central Somalia.

The group has exerted temporary and, at times, sustained control over strategic locations in those areas by recruiting, sometimes forcibly, regional sub-clans and their militias, using guerrilla warfare and terrorist tactics against the Somali Federal Government (SFG), African Union Mission in Somalia (AMISOM) peacekeepers, and nongovernmental aid organizations. As of 2013, however, pressure from AMISOM and Ethiopian forces had largely degraded al-Shabaab's control, especially in Mogadishu but also in other key regions of the country, and conflict among senior leaders has exacerbated fractures within the group. In 2013 al-Shabaab rivalries culminated in a major purge of opponents of deceased group leader Ahmed Abdi Aw-Mohamed.

Al-Shabaab is not centralized or monolithic in its agenda or goals. Its rank-and-file members come from disparate clans, and the group is susceptible to clan politics, internal divisions, and shifting alliances. Most of its fighters are predominantly interested in the nationalistic battle against the SFG and not supportive of global jihad. Al-Shabaab's senior leaders are affiliated with al-Qa'ida and are believed to have trained and fought in Afghanistan. The merger of the two groups was publicly announced in February 2012 by the amir of al-Shabaab and Ayman al-Zawahiri, leader of al-Qa'ida.

Al-Shabaab has claimed responsibility for many bombings—including various types of suicide attacks—in Mogadishu and in central and northern Somalia, typically targeting Somali government officials, AMISOM, and perceived allies of the SFG. Since 2013 al-Shabaab has launched high-profile operations in neighboring countries, most notably the September 2013 Westgate Mall attack in Nairobi and the May 2014 attack against a restaurant in Djibouti popular with Westerners. The Westgate attack killed 67 Kenyan and non-Kenyan nationals, and a siege continued at the mall for several days.

Al-Shabaab claimed responsibility for the twin suicide bombings in Kampala, Uganda, on 11 July 2010 that killed more than 70 people, as well as a June 2013 attack in Mogadishu on a United Nations compound, which killed 22 people. A February 2014 al-Shabaab attack on Somalia's presidential palace, Villa Somalia, involved a car bomb and armed assailants and killed 12 people, nine of them militants. In June 2014, an attack and siege in Mpeketoni, Kenya, killed nearly 50 tourists; although there was no claim of responsibility, al-Shabaab was widely believed responsible. There were other high-profile attacks in 2014 either ascribed to or claimed by al-Shabaab.

Ansar al-Sharia

Ansar al-Sharia groups in Libya emerged following the 2011 Libyan revolution. Their goal is to establish sharia and to remove US and Western influence from Libya. Ansar al-Sharia has nodes in Libyan cities that work with regional extremist groups to train, conduct attacks, and amass weapons. The term Ansar al-Sharia means "Partisans of Islamic Law."

Ansar al-Sharia in Benghazi (AAS-B) and in Darnah (AAS-D) were most likely involved in the 11 September 2012 attacks against US facilities in Benghazi that resulted in the death of J. Christopher Stevens, the US Ambassador to Libya, and three other US citizens. The United States designated AAS-B and AAS-D as Foreign Terrorist Organizations in January 2014. The groups are also suspected of involvement in attacks and kidnappings targeting foreigners, including the assassination of an American teacher in Benghazi in December 2013.

Muhammad al-Zahawi is widely recognized as AAS's amir and spiritual leader. He stated in a December 2013 news interview that the group continued to reject any form of government other than sharia and that the government should consult the Qur'an on all matters. Al-Zahawi publicly rejects any association between AAS and al-Qa'ida.

Ansar al-Sharia in Tunisia (AAS-T) was blamed for inciting the storming of the US Embassy in Tunis on 14 September 2012, and has since been designated by the United States as a Foreign Terrorist Organization. AAS-T remains intent on conducting attacks against Western interests in spite of increasing Tunisian security capability and counterterrorism operations. AAS-T attempted suicide attacks against two tourist sites in October 2013 and in 2014 probably has been plotting against Jewish targets and Western diplomatic missions in Tunisia.

Al-Qa'ida
in the Arabian Peninsula (AQAP)

Al-Qa'ida in the Arabian Peninsula (AQAP) is a Sunni extremist group based in Yemen that has orchestrated numerous high-profile terrorist attacks. One of the most notable of these operations occurred when AQAP dispatched Nigerian-born Umar Farouk Abdulmutallab, who attempted to detonate an explosive device aboard a Northwest Airlines flight on 25 December 2009—the first attack inside the United States by an al-Qa'ida affiliate since 11 September 2001. That was followed by an attempted attack in which explosive-laden packages were sent to the United States on 27 October 2010. The year 2010 also saw the launch of Inspire magazine, an AQAP-branded, English-language publication that first appeared in July, followed by the establishment of AQAP's Arabic-language al-Madad News Agency in 2011. Dual US-Yemeni citizen Anwar al-Aulaqi, who had a worldwide following as a radical ideologue and propagandist, was the most prominent member

In August 2013, the US State Department temporarily closed several embassies in response to a threat associated with AQAP. Since then, AQAP has conducted a number of high-profile attacks inside Yemen targeting the Yemeni Government, including a complex, multistage attack in December 2013 against Yemen's Ministry of Defense that killed at least 52 people, and in February 2014 the group freed over two dozen prisoners after attacking Sanaa's central prison. Shortly thereafter the group released a video entitled "Drops of Rain," which depicted a large gathering of AQAP members operating openly while their leader threatened the United States. In May 2014, the US Embassy in Sanaa closed for a month due to a heightened threat from the group.

AQAP's predecessor, al-Qa'ida in Yemen (AQY), came into existence after the escape of 23 al-Qa'ida members from prison in Sanaa, in February 2006. Several escapees helped reestablish the group and later identified fellow escapee al-Wahishi as the group's new amir.

AQY in early 2008 dramatically increased its operational tempo, carrying out small-arms attacks on foreign tourists and a series of mortar attacks against the US and Italian Embassies in Sanaa, the presidential compound, and Yemeni military complexes. In September 2008 the group attacked the US Embassy in

Sanaa using two vehicle bombs that detonated outside the compound, killing 19 people.

AQAP emerged in January 2009 following an announcement that Yemeni and Saudi terrorists were unifying under a common banner. The leadership of this new organization was composed of the group's amir, Nasir al-Wahishi; now-deceased deputy amir Sa'id al-Shahri; and military commander Qasim al-Rimi, all veteran extremist leaders. The group has targeted local, US, and Western interests in the Arabian Peninsula, but is now pursuing a global strategy. AQAP elements withdrew from their southern Yemen strongholds in June 2012, when Yemeni military forces under new President Abdu Rabbo Mansour Hadi—with the support of local tribesmen—regained control of cities in Abyan and Shabwah that had served as AQAP strongholds since 2011.

Al-Qa'ida in the Lands
of the Islamic Maghreb (AQIM)

Al-Qa'ida in the Lands of the Islamic Maghreb (AQIM) is an Algeria-based Sunni Muslim jihadist group. It originally formed in 1998 as the Salafist Group for Preaching and Combat (GSPC), a faction of the Armed Islamic Group, which was the largest and most active terrorist group in Algeria. The GSPC was renamed in January 2007 after the group officially joined al-Qa'ida in September 2006. The group had close to 30,000 members at its height, but the Algerian Government's counterterrorism efforts have reduced GSPC's ranks to fewer than 1,000. The current leader of AQIM is Abdelmalek Droukdal, who has been in charge of AQIM since it was founded in 1998 as the GSPC.

AQIM historically has operated primarily in the northern coastal areas of Algeria and in parts of the desert regions of southern Algeria and the Sahel. Since the French-led military intervention in early 2013, however, the group has reduced its presence in northern Mali and expanded into Libya and Tunisia. AQIM mainly employs conventional terrorist tactics, including guerrilla-style ambushes, mortar, rocket, and IED attacks. The group's principal sources of revenue include extortion, kidnapping for ransom, and donations. In May 2009, AQIM announced it had killed a British hostage after months of failed negotiations. In June of the same year, the group publicly claimed responsibility for killing US citizen Christopher Leggett in Mauritania because of his missionary activities. In 2011, a Mauritanian court sentenced a suspected AQIM member to death and two others to prison for the American's murder.

AQIM since 2010 has failed to conduct the high-casualty attacks in Algeria that it had in previous years. Multinational counterterrorism efforts—including a joint French-Mauritanian raid in July 2010 against an AQIM camp—resulted in the death of some AQIM members and possibly disrupted some AQIM activity. In 2011, however, AQIM killed two French hostages during an attempted rescue operation, and in 2013 killed one French hostage in retaliation for France's military intervention in Mali. AQIM continues to hold five French, one South African, one Dutch, and one Swede hostage.

In 2012, AQIM took advantage of political chaos in northern Mali to consolidate its control there and worked with the secular Azawad National Liberation Movement (MNLA) to secure independence in Kidal, Gao, and Timbuktu for ethnic Tuaregs. The Islamic militant group Ansar al-Dine was formed to support the creation of an Islamic state in Mali ruled by sharia.

Since 2011, dissident groups of AQIM members broke away to form Movement for Unity and Jihad in West Africa (MUJAO) and al-Mulathamun Battalion and its subordinate unit al-Muwaqi'un Bil-Dima ("Those Who Sign With Blood") led by former AQIM battalion leader Mokhtar Belmokhtar. In August 2013 these groups merged to form al-Murabitun, ("The Sentinels"), and officially formalized the groups' ties; their stated goals are to "unite all Muslims from the Nile to the Atlantic in jihad against Westerners" and to curb French influence in the region.

Al-Qa'ida

Established by Usama Bin Ladin in 1988 with Arabs who fought in Afghanistan against the Soviet Union, al-Qa'ida's declared goal is the establishment of a pan-Islamic caliphate throughout the Muslim world. Toward this end, al-Qa'ida seeks to unite Muslims to fight the West, especially the United States, as a means of overthrowing Muslim regimes al-Qa'ida deems "apostate," expelling Western influence from Muslim countries, and defeating Israel. Al-Qa'ida issued a statement in February 1998 under the banner of "the World Islamic Front for Jihad Against the Jews and Crusaders" saying it was the duty of all Muslims to kill US citizens—civilian and military—and their allies everywhere. The group merged with the Egyptian Islamic Jihad (al-Jihad) in June 2001.

On 11 September 2001, 19 al-Qa'ida suicide attackers hijacked and crashed four US commercial jets—two into the World Trade Center in New York City, one into the Pentagon near Washington, D.C., and a fourth into a field in Shanksville, Pennsylvania—leaving nearly 3,000 people dead. Al-Qa'ida also directed the 12 October 2000 attack on the USS Cole in the port of Aden, Yemen, which killed 17 US sailors and injured another 39, and conducted the bombings in August 1998 of the US embassies in Nairobi, Kenya, and Dar es Salaam, Tanzania, killing 224 people and injuring more than 5,000. Since 2002, al-Qa'ida and affiliated groups have conducted attacks worldwide, including in Europe, North Africa, South Asia, Southeast Asia, and the Middle East.

In 2005, Ayman al-Zawahiri, then Bin Ladin's deputy and now the leader of al-Qa'ida, publicly claimed al-Qa'ida's involvement in the 7 July 2005 bus bombings in the United Kingdom. In 2006, British security services foiled an al-Qa'ida plot to detonate explosives on up to 10 transatlantic flights originating from London's Heathrow airport. During that same time period, numbers of al-Qa'ida-affiliated groups increased.

Following the 2011 death of Bin Ladin, al-Qa'ida leaders moved quickly to name al-Zawahiri as his successor. The group remains a cohesive organization and what is widely called al-Qa'ida's Core leadership continues to be important to the global movement despite leadership losses. Other jihadist groups, however, like the Islamic State of Iraq and the Levant (ISIL), have gained prominence and challenged the Core's global leadership.

Al-Qa'ida remains committed to conducting attacks in the United States and against American interests abroad. The group has advanced a number of unsuccessful plots in the past several years, including against the United States and Europe. This highlights al-Qa'ida's ability to continue some attack preparations while under sustained counterterrorism pressure and suggests it may be plotting additional attacks against the United States at home or overseas.

Moving forward into 2015, the group could seek to reconstitute the remnants of the group in Afghanistan. Al-Qa'ida's historical ties to Afghanistan make the country an attractive operating area, especially if the group can leverage its longstanding relationships with Afghan insurgents who supported it in the years preceding 9/11.

Imirat Kavkaz

Imirat Kavkaz, (IK, or Caucasus Emirate), founded in late 2007 by now-deceased Chechen extremist Doku Umarov, is an Islamist militant organization based in Russia's North Caucasus. Its stated goal is the liberation of what it considers to be Muslim lands from Moscow. The group, now led by Ali Abu-Muhammad, also known as Aliaskhab Kebekov, regularly conducts attacks against Russian security forces in the North Caucasus. In the period 2010-2011, it carried out high-profile suicide bombings against civilian targets in Moscow that killed dozens. IK maintains ties with militants from the North Caucasus fighting alongside groups aiming to topple Bashar al-Asad in Syria.

In the approach to the Sochi Olympic Games, Umarov on 2 July 2013 urged militants in Russia to target the Games, stating that Moscow "plan[s] to hold the Olympics on the bones of our ancestors, on the bones of many dead Muslims...and we mujahedin are obliged not to permit that." While there were attacks in Volgograd in the weeks before the event that killed more than 30 civilians, no attacks took place on site during the Games. The US State Department in May 2011 designated Imirat Kavkaz as a Specially Designated Terrorist group under Executive Order 13224.

The Islamic Jihad Union (IJU) is an extremist organization that splintered from the Islamic Movement of Uzbekistan in the early 2000s and is currently based in Pakistan's Federally Administered Tribal Areas. The IJU, which is committed to toppling the government in Uzbekistan, conducted two attacks there in 2004 and one in 2009. The IJU is also active in Afghanistan, where the group operates alongside the Taliban-affiliated Haqqani Network. The group has had particular success in recruiting German nationals and achieved international notoriety following the 2007 disruption of an IJU plot by the so-called Sauerland Cell to attack various targets in Germany. The US State Department in June 2005 designated the IJU a Foreign Terrorist Organization.

The Islamic Movement of Uzbekistan (IMU) is an extremist organization that formed in the late 1990s and is currently based in Pakistan's Federally Administered Tribal Areas. The IMU seeks to overthrow the government in Uzbekistan and establish a radical Islamist caliphate in all of "Turkestan," which it considers to be the Central Asian region between the Caspian Sea and Xinjiang in western China. The IMU has become increasingly active in the

Taliban-led insurgency in northern Afghanistan, providing the IMU with a springboard for future operations in Central Asia. A known IMU spokesperson in a video message delivered to Radio Liberty's Tajik service claimed responsibility for a September 2010 ambush against a military convoy in Tajikistan. The IMU in June 2014 joined Tehrik-e Taliban Pakistan fighters in a deadly siege of Karachi International Airport that killed 37.

Boko Haram

Boko Haram, which refers to itself as "Jama'atu Ahl as-Sunnah li-Da'awati wal-Jihad" (JASDJ; Group of the Sunni People for the Calling and Jihad) and "Nigerian Taliban"—other translations and variants are used—is a Nigeria-based group that seeks to overthrow the current Nigerian Government and replace it with a regime based on Islamic law. It is popularly known in Nigerian and Western media as "Boko Haram," which means "Western education is forbidden" (the word boko is a holdover from the colonial English word for book). The group, which has existed in various forms since the late 1990s, suffered setbacks in July 2009 when clashes with Nigerian Government forces led to the deaths of hundreds of its members, including former leader Muhammad Yusuf.

In July 2010, Boko Haram's former second-in-command, Abubakar Shekau, appeared in a video claiming leadership of the group and threatening attacks on Western influences in Nigeria. Later that month, Shekau issued a second statement expressing solidarity with al-Qa'ida and threatening the United States. Under Shekau's leadership, the group has continued to demonstrate growing operational capabilities, with an increasing use of improvised explosive device (IED) attacks against soft targets. The group set off its first vehicle-borne IED in June 2011. On 26 August 2011, Boko Haram conducted its first attack against a Western interest—a vehicle-bomb attack on UN headquarters in Abuja—killing at least 23 people and injuring more than 80. A purported Boko Haram spokesman claimed responsibility for the attack and promised future targeting of US and Nigerian Government interests.

Boko Haram's capability has increased in 2014, with the group conducting near-daily attacks against a wide range of targets, including Christians, Nigerian security and police forces, the media, schools, politicians, and Muslims perceived as collaborators. Boko Haram continues to expand its activity into neighboring countries and has claimed responsibility for the kidnapping of 11 Westerners in Cameroon since early 2013, raising the group's international profile and emphasizing the growing threat it poses to Western and regional interests.

Boko Haram's unprecedented levels of violence—including the kidnapping of 276 schoolgirls in Borno State, Nigeria, in April 2014—have brought international condemnation as well as collaboration on security initiatives by the United States, United Kingdom, France, African partners, and others as Nigerian and other regional security forces continue to try to oust the group from northeastern Nigeria and its safe havens throughout the area.

Hezb-e-Islami

Hezb-e-Islami, or "Party of Islam," is a political and paramilitary organization in Afghanistan founded in 1976 by former Afghan prime minister Gulbuddin Hekmatyar, who has been prominent in various Afghan conflicts since the late 1970s. Hezb-e Islami Gulbuddin (HIG) is an offshoot of that original Hezb-e-Islami, and is a virulently anti-Western insurgent group whose goal is to replace the Western-backed Afghan Government with an Islamic state rooted in sharia in line with Hekmatyar's vision of a Pashtun-dominated Afghanistan. His group conducts attacks against Coalition forces, Afghan Government targets, and Western interests in Afghanistan. HIG is distinct from Hezb-e-Islami Afghanistan (HIA), a legal Afghan political party composed of, among others, some reconciled HIG members. HIG shares most elements of Taliban ideology and HIG insurgents cooperate with the Taliban in some parts of Afghanistan despite some ideological differences.

Hekmatyar and his deputies, Ghairat Baheer and Qutbuddin Hilal, continue to participate sporadically in negotiations with the Afghan Government. Hilal even ran for Afghan president in the country's April 2014 election. HIG, however, strongly opposes the proposed Bilateral Security Agreement with the United States and, after Hilal's failed presidential bid, boycotted the subsequent election run-off.

The group has conducted some widely publicized attacks during the past few years even while negotiations were under way. Most recently, HIG spokesman Haroon Zarghoon claimed responsibility for a suicide VBIED attack in Kabul on 10 February 2014, which killed at least two US civilians and wounded two other Americans and seven Afghan nationals. HIG was also responsible for a 16 May 2013 suicide VBIED attack in Kabul, which destroyed a US armored SUV and killed two US soldiers, four US civilian contractors, eight Afghans—including two children—and wounded at least 37 others. The attack marked the deadliest incident against US personnel in Kabul in over a year.

Jaish-e-Mohammed

Jaish-e-Mohammed (JEM)—also known as the Army of Mohammed, Khudamul Islam, and Tehrik ul-Furqaan among other names—is an extremist group based in Pakistan. It was founded by Masood Azhar in early 2000 upon his release from prison in India. The group's aim is to unite Kashmir with Pakistan and to expel foreign troops from Afghanistan. JEM has openly declared war against the United States. Pakistan outlawed JEM in 2002, and by 2003 JEM had splintered into Khuddam ul-Islam (KUI), headed by Azhar, and Jamaat ul-Furqan (JUF), led by Abdul Jabbar. Pakistani authorities detained Abdul Jabbar for suspected involvement in the December 2003 assassination attempts against President Pervez Musharraf but released him in August 2004. Pakistan banned KUI and JUF in November 2003.

JEM continues to operate openly in parts of Pakistan despite the 2002 ban on its activities. Since JEM founder Masood Azhar's release in 2000, JEM has conducted many lethal terrorist attacks, including a suicide bombing of the Jammu and Kashmir legislative assembly building in the Indian-administered Kashmir capital of Srinagar in October 2001 that killed more than 30. In July 2004, Pakistani authorities arrested a JEM member wanted in connection with the 2002 abduction and murder of US journalist Daniel Pearl.

In 2006 JEM claimed responsibility for a number of attacks, including the killing of several Indian police officials in Srinagar. JEM members also were involved in the 2007 Red Mosque uprising in Islamabad. Asmatullah Moavia, a militant currently associated with Tehrik-e Taliban Pakistan, split from the group after the Red Mosque incident because of disagreements over how to react to it. In 2009, Pakistani authorities detained several JEM members suspected of taking part in a 3 March attack on the Sri Lankan cricket team in Lahore.

In June 2008, JEM reportedly was working to resolve its differences with other Pakistani extremist groups and began shifting its focus from Kashmir to Afghanistan in order to step up attacks against US and Coalition forces. Rogue factions of JEM, in conjunction with other regional groups, may conduct attacks against Western interests in Pakistan as well as attack Pakistani Government entities.

JEM has at least several hundred armed supporters located in Pakistan, India's southern Kashmir and Doda regions, and in the Kashmir Valley. Supporters are mostly Pakistanis and Kashmiris, but also include Afghans and Arab veterans of the Afghan war against the Soviets. The group uses light and heavy machine guns, assault rifles, mortars, improvised explosive devices, and rocket-propelled grenades in its attacks.

Jemaah Islamiyah

Jemaah Islamiyah (JI) is an Indonesia-based clandestine terrorist network formed in the early 1990s to establish an Islamic state encompassing southern Thailand, Malaysia, Singapore, Indonesia, Brunei, and the southern Philippines. Its operatives, who trained in camps in Afghanistan and the southern Philippines, began conducting attacks in 1999. The network's existence was discovered in late 2001 after Singaporean authorities disrupted a cell that was planning to attack targets associated with the US Navy.

JI is responsible for a series of lethal bombings targeting Western interests in Indonesia and the Philippines from 2000-2005, including attacks in 2002 against two nightclubs in Bali that killed 202 people; the 2003 car bombing of the JW Marriott hotel in Jakarta that killed 12; the 2004 truck bombing of the Australian Embassy that killed 11; and the 2005 suicide bombing of three establishments in Bali that killed 22. A JI splinter group led by Noordin Mat Top in July 2009 conducted suicide bombings at two hotels in Jakarta.

Southeast Asian governments since 2002 have arrested more than 300 suspected terrorists, significantly degrading JI's network. Thai authorities detained the network's operations chief in 2003. Indonesian police killed JI's most experienced bombmaker in 2005 and arrested its two senior leaders in mid-2007. Malaysian authorities arrested two senior JI operatives in Kuala Lumpur in early 2008 and in April 2009 recaptured fugitive Singapore JI leader Mas Selamat Kasteri, who escaped from his Singaporean prison cell in early 2008. Indonesian police in September 2009 killed Noordin Mat Top.

Since 2009, JI has been overshadowed by the activities of its splinter groups and other Indonesia-based terrorists, some of whom are experienced operatives previously affiliated with JI; others are convicted terrorists who completed prison sentences and have since resumed their activities. Indonesian terrorist Umar Patek—arrested by Pakistani authorities in Abbotabad in January 2011 and repatriated seven months later—was convicted in June 2012 for his role in the 2002 Bali bombings and sentenced to 20 years in prison. In November 2012, Philippine security forces killed senior Indonesian JI leader Sanusi.

Lashkar-e-Tayyiba

Lashkar-e-Tayyiba (LT), also known as Army of the Righteous, is one of the largest and most proficient of the Kashmir-focused militant groups. LT formed in the early 1990s as the military wing of Markaz-ud-Dawa-wal-Irshad, a Pakistan-based Islamic fundamentalist missionary organization founded in the 1980s to oppose the Soviets in Afghanistan. Since 1993, LT has conducted numerous attacks against Indian troops and civilian targets in the disputed Jammu and Kashmir state, as well as several high-profile attacks inside India itself. Concern over new LT attacks in India remains high.

The United States and United Nations have designated LT as an international terrorist organization. The Pakistani Government banned LT and froze its assets in 2002. In June 2014, the US Treasury Department imposed sanctions on two additional LT leaders and the US State Department amended the Foreign Terrorist Organizations and Specially Designated Global Terrorist designations for LT to include four additional front organizations. In April 2012 two senior LT leaders were designated by the US State Department Rewards for Justice program.

The Indian Government has charged LT with committing the 26–29 November 2008 attacks in Mumbai, in which gunmen using automatic weapons and grenades attacked several sites, killing more than 160 people. Pakistani authorities have detained and are prosecuting several LT leaders for the Mumbai attacks. David Headley, an American citizen who acknowledged attending LT training camps, pleaded guilty in March 2010 to scouting targets for the Mumbai attacks. On 21 November 2012, India executed the lone surviving Mumbai attacker—Ajmal Kasab, a Pakistani—after the Indian Supreme Court upheld his death sentence. India has accused LT of involvement in other high-profile attacks, including the 11 July 2006 attack on multiple Mumbai commuter trains that killed more than 180 people, and the December 2001 armed assault on the Indian Parliament building that left 12 dead. Afghan and US officials have blamed LT for the May 2014 attack on the Indian consulate in Herat, Afghanistan.

LT's exact size is unknown, but the group probably has several thousand members. Elements of LT are active in Afghanistan and the group also recruits internationally, as evidenced by the arrest in the United States of Jubair Ahmed in 2011, Headley's arrest in 2009, and the indictment of 11 LT terrorists in Virginia in 2003. LT maintains facilities in Pakistan, including training camps, schools, and medical clinics. In March 2002, senior al-Qa'ida lieutenant Abu Zubaydah was captured at an LT safehouse in Faisalabad, suggesting that some LT members assist the group.

LT coordinates its charitable activities through its front organization, Jamaat-ud-Dawa (JuD), which spearheaded humanitarian relief to the victims of the October 2005 earthquake in Kashmir. JuD activities, however, have been limited since December 2008 by the UN's designation of the group as an alias for LT. During the 2010 floods in Pakistan, JuD and an affiliated charity, the Falah-i-Insaniyat Foundation (FiF), were widely reported to have provided aid to flood victims. In 2014, JuD and FiF were providing relief to internally displaced persons in Pakistan who fled from Pakistani military operations in the Federally Administered Tribal Areas.

Lashkar-e-Jhangvi

Lashkar-e-Jhangvi (LJ) was founded in 1996 as a militant offshoot of Sipah-i-Sahaba Pakistan, a Deobandi and anti-Shia group that emerged in the mid-1980s in reaction to class-based conflict and the domestic Pakistani Shia revival that followed the Iranian revolution. LJ seeks to transform Pakistan into a Deobandi-dominated Sunni state, and primarily targets Shia and other religious minorities.

Akram Lahori is the leader of LJ but in 2002 was arrested, later convicted of sectarian killings, and is currently incarcerated. Lahori officially remains LJ's amir and Malik Mohammad Ishaq, one of LJ's founding members, is believed to have taken command since his release from prison in 2011. According to Pakistani media reporting, LJ consists of at least eight loosely coordinated cells spread across Pakistan with independent chiefs for each cell. At least seven of these cells—Lashkar-e-Jhangvi Al Alami, Asif Chotoo group, Akram Lahori group, Naeem Bukhari group, Qari Zafar group, Qari Shakeel group, and Farooq Bengali group—are active in Pakistan's largest city, Karachi. Many are linked to al-Qa'ida and Tehrik-e Taliban Pakistan (TTP) but still recognize Ishaq as the head of LJ. In particular, LJ cells also often coordinate with TTP factions in Karachi when targeting law enforcement agencies and Shia.

LJ collaborates and has overlapping membership with other Pakistan-based radical Sunni groups including al-Qa'ida and TTP. Pakistani authorities suspected LJ collaborated with these groups in the 2009 attack on the Pakistan Army General Headquarters in Islamabad and in several attacks in 2010 targeting Pakistan's Criminal Investigation Department. LJ members reportedly also have been linked to a number of high-profile kidnappings and killings of Westerners in the region, such as the 1997 killing of four US oil workers in Karachi, the 2002 kidnapping and execution of US journalist Daniel Pearl, the August 2010 kidnapping of the son-in-law of the former Chairman of the Joint Chiefs of Staff Committee, and the August 2011 kidnapping of a US citizen that was later publicly claimed by al-Qa'ida.

In 2013, LJ claimed credit for some of the most deadly sectarian attacks in Pakistan's history. In January, a billiard hall in Quetta, Balochistan Province, was hit by two blasts, first by a suicide bomber and about 10 minutes later by a car bomb, killing 92 people and injuring more than 120, mostly Shia. In February, explosives hidden in a water tanker exploded in a crowded market in Hazara town, a Shia-dominated area on the edge of Quetta. The blast killed 81 people and wounded 178, stoking anger and frustration among Shia at the authorities' inability or unwillingness to crack down on LJ. The group, with al-Qa'ida, also claimed responsibility for a June suicide attack in Quetta against a bus carrying Pakistani female university students. A female suicide bomber was one of the attackers, and at least 25 people were killed, which included a follow-on assault on a nearby hospital.

TEHRIK-E TALIBAN PAKISTAN

The Taliban is a Sunni Islamist nationalist and pro-Pashtun movement founded in the early 1990s that ruled most of Afghanistan from 1996 until October 2001. The movement's founding nucleus—the word "Taliban" is Pashto for "students"—was composed of peasant farmers and men studying Islam in Afghan and Pakistani madrasas, or religious schools. The Taliban found a foothold and consolidated their strength in southern Afghanistan.

By 1994, the Taliban had moved their way through the south, capturing several provinces from various armed factions who had been fighting a civil war after the Soviet-backed Afghan government fell in 1992. The Taliban's first move was to institute a strict interpretation of Qur'anic instruction and jurisprudence. In practice, this meant often merciless policies on the treatment of women, political opponents of any type, and religious minorities.

Tehrik-e Taliban Pakistan (TTP) is an alliance of militant networks formed in 2007 to unify opposition against the Pakistani military. TTP's stated objectives are the expulsion of Islamabad's influence in the Federally Administered Tribal Areas and neighboring Khyber Pakhtunkhwa Province in Pakistan, the implementation of a strict interpretation of sharia throughout Pakistan, and the expulsion of Coalition troops from Afghanistan. TTP leaders also publicly say that the group seeks to establish an Islamic caliphate in Pakistan that would require the overthrow of the Pakistani Government. TTP historically maintained close ties to senior al-Qa'ida leaders, including al-Qa'ida's former head of operations for Pakistan.

Baitullah Mehsud, the first TTP leader, died on 5 August 2009, and his successor, Hakimullah Mehsud, died on 1 November 2013. TTP's central shura in November 2013 appointed Mullah Fazlullah as the group's overall leader. Fazlullah is staunchly anti-Western, anti-Islamabad, and advocates harsh tactics underscored by his ordering the November 2012 attempted assassination of education rights activist Malala Yousafzai. TTP since 2008 has repeatedly publicly threatened to attack the US homeland, and a TTP spokesman claimed responsibility for the failed vehicle-bomb attack in Times Square, New York City, on 1 May 2010. In June 2011, a spokesman vowed to attack the United States and Europe in revenge for the death of Usama Bin Ladin. A TTP leader in April 2012 endorsed external operations by the group and threatened attacks in the United Kingdom for its involvement in Afghanistan.

Al-Murabitun

Al-Murabitun, which seeks to "unite all Muslims from the Nile to the Atlantic in jihad against Westerners" and "liberate Mali from France," according to the group's public announcement, was formed when veteran jihadist Mokhtar Belmokhtar in August 2013 merged his al-Mulathamun Battalion with Al-Tawhid Wal Jihad in West Africa (TWJWA). The merger formalized an already close relationship between two of the most active terrorist groups in North and West Africa. The two groups—both offshoots of al-Qa'ida in the Lands of the Islamic Maghreb (AQIM)—conducted numerous attacks against Westerners in North and West Africa prior to their merger, including the January 2013 attack on the I-n-Amenas gas facility in Algeria that killed nearly 40 Westerners, including three Americans, and a joint operation in May 2013 in Niger simultaneously targeting a French uranium mine and a Nigerian military barracks.

French CT operations have killed at least four senior leaders and dozens of rank-and-file members of al-Murabitun—including its titular leader, Abu Bakr al-Masri—in Mali since November 2013, possibly preventing the group from carrying out a high-profile attack in the region. However, al-Murabitun has conducted small-scale but lethal attacks against UN targets in Mali and remains the most potent threat in the Sahel because of Belmokhtar's anti-West agenda and vast network of extremists. In its initial announcement, the new group pledged allegiance to al-Qa'ida senior leadership and its commitment to the philosophy of jihad put forward by Usama Bin Ladin, suggesting a focus on anti-Western attacks, and in two separate statements in 2014 the group reaffirmed its allegiance to Ayman al-Zawahiri and restated its intent to continue to attack France and its allies.

Al-Mulathamun Battalion and its subordinate unit, al-Muwaqi'un Bil-Dima ("Those Who Sign With Blood"), led by Mokhtar Belmokhtar, splintered from AQIM in fall 2012 due to leadership disputes. Belmokhtar has a long history of jihadist activity in North and West Africa dating back almost two decades. He fought with the mujahidin in Afghanistan as a teenager and trained with al-Qa'ida, where he lost an eye mishandling explosives. By the late 1990s, Belmokhtar seized control over lucrative trans-Saharan smuggling routes, reportedly earning millions by trafficking cigarettes.

Tawhid Wal Jihad in West Africa (TWJWA), also known as the Movement for Unity and Jihad in West Africa (MUJAO), was founded in late 2011 as an offshoot of AQIM and has coordinated terrorist attacks across North and West Africa. Since the French-led intervention in Mali began in mid-January 2013, TWJWA has conducted a majority of the attacks targeting French and African forces in the vicinity of Gao and Kidal, using suicide bombings, vehicle-borne improvised explosive devices, and landmines.

Al-Murabitun, an Arabic phrase meaning "The Sentinels," invokes a medieval dynasty of the same name—known in English as the Almoravids—that originated as a religious and military movement and whose nomadic founders emerged from present-day Western Sahara in the mid-11th century. The Almoravids ruled much of northwest Africa and southern Spain for nearly 100 years, professing a rigorous Islamic creed and imposing a strict form of sharia on the peoples they conquered.